THIS *Book* BELONGS TO

....

PLATYPUS EXPERT

For Vera & Eva

© 2022 South Sound Unlimited

No part of this publication may be reproduced, stored in a retrieval system, or transmitted in any form or by any means, electronic, mechanical, photocopying, recording, or otherwise, without written permission of the publisher.

For information, email kate@southsoundunlimited.com

Hello! Platypus

a

Hello! Zoology

book

by Kate Perez

1

Hello! I am a platypus.

See the meaning of words in GREEN at the end of the book!

I am a special kind of mammal called a monotreme.

Ornithorhynchus anatinus

Age: Up to 20 years

Length: About 20 inches

Weight: 2-4 lbs

Colors: brown, tan, black

3

I only live

in one part of the world...

Eastern Australia!

5

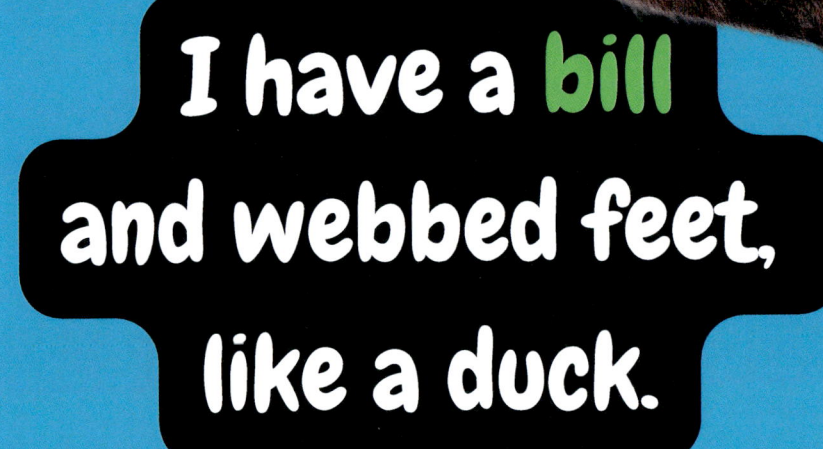

I have a **bill** and webbed feet, like a duck.

20 inches

I am about the size of a house cat.

I have a wide tail, like a beaver.

7

My fur helps me stay warm under water.

My fur is **biofluorescent** ...

My bill is soft and leathery.

...it glows blue and green under **ultraviolet** light.

8

I live in a burrow

I hide the entrance to my burrow in long grass or even under water.

down by the river.

I make my burrow cozy with soft dirt and leaves.

10

11

Brushtail Possom

Sugar Glider

Tasmanian Devil

Rainbow Lorikeet

I have lots of

Koala

Long-necked Turtle

Echidna

Kangaroo

Flying Fox

Wallaby

cool neighbors.

G'day!

Kookaburra

12

13

When I see these predators I run or hide!

Fox

Eagle

Goanna

River Rat

Crocodile

Python

14

I am an excellent swimmer.

I paddle with my webbed feet.

My bill has **electroreception** to help me sense what is in the water.

I am very slow on land!

16

17

Platy-paddle!

Swan dive!

I am mainly nocturnal.

Back stroke!

I spend up to eleven hours each night swimming and **foraging** for food.

18

19

I am a carnivore.

water bugs

shrimp

I eat small animals from the river bed.

insect larvae

worms

I need to eat one-fifth of my body weight each day.

20

21

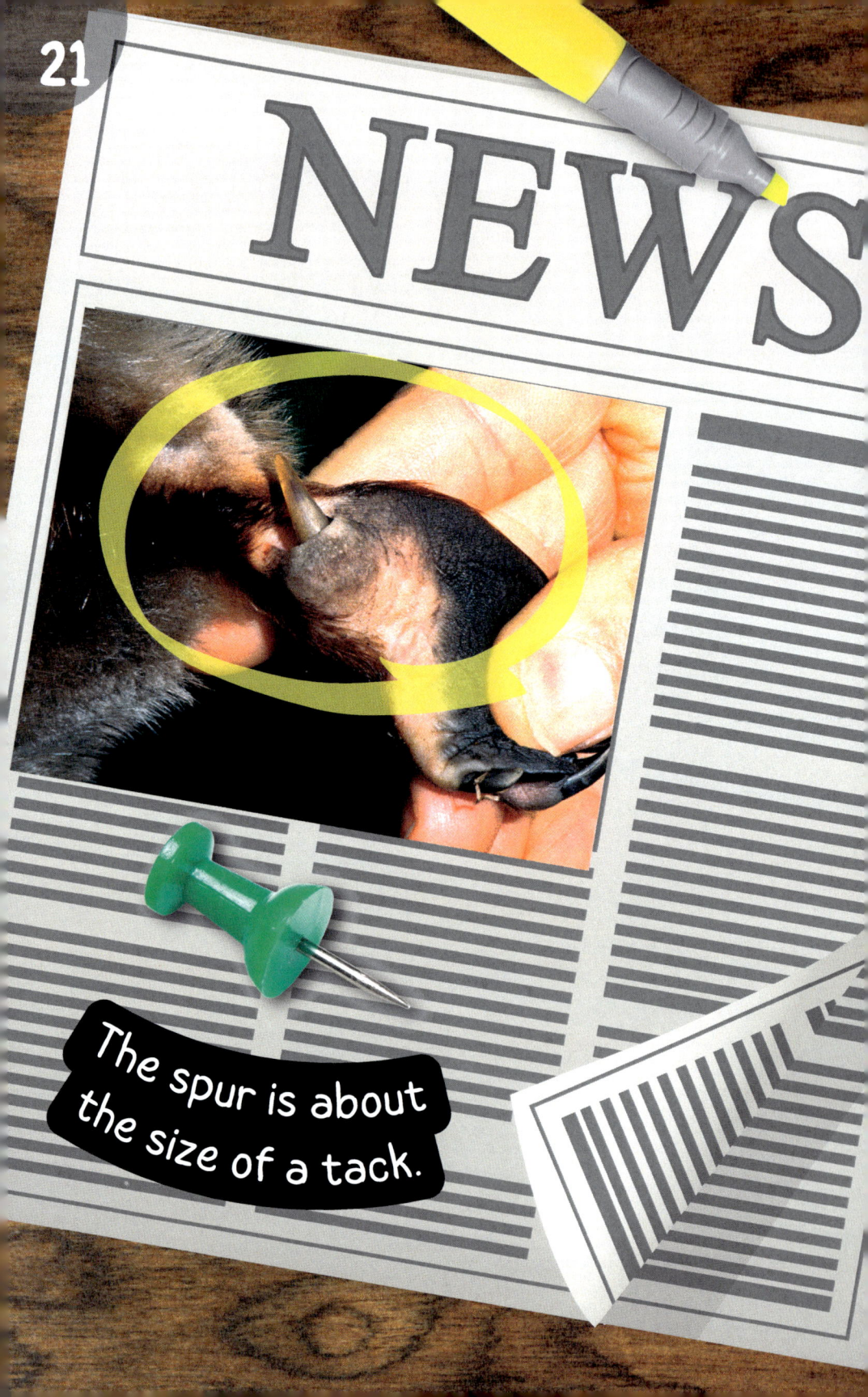

NEWS

The spur is about the size of a tack.

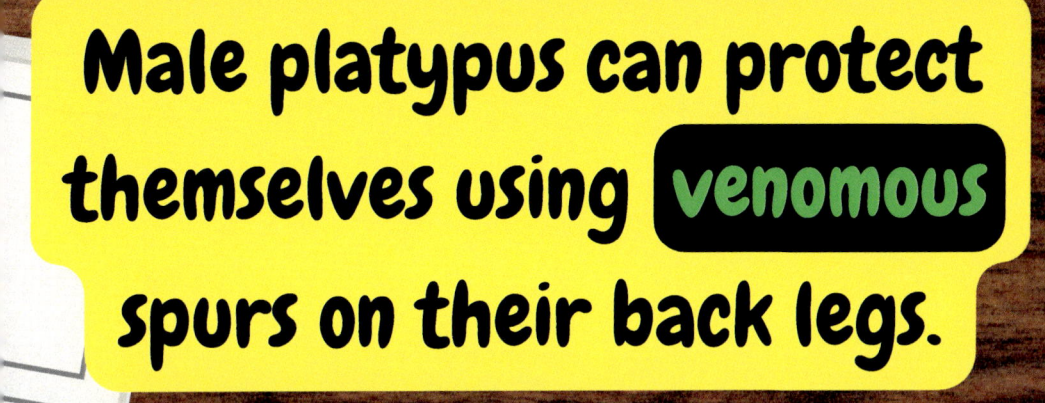

Male platypus can protect themselves using `venomous` spurs on their back legs.

The venom only causes pain to humans, but it is enough to kill a small animal.

23

A mother platypus lays eggs in her burrow.

Platypus babies are called puggles!

The puggles remain in the

The mom **incubates** the eggs for around 10 days.

The eggs have soft, leathery shells.

burrow for 3-4 months.

24

Platypus are listed as **Near Threatened** ...

...because there are fewer than there once was.

Habitat loss is our biggest threat.

27

You can meet a platypus...

...at the San Diego Zoo...

There are about 28 platypus in **captivity**. Only two are outside of Australia!

...or at a zoo in Australia.

29

The platypus is one of only two egg-laying mammals, called monotremes.

Some zoos keep platypus in the dark during the day and light at night so the platypus are active when the zoo is open.

It takes much more energy for a platypus to walk on land than to swim.

Mom platypus use wet leaves and grass to keep their eggs from drying out.

The platypus is so odd that when it was first discovered, some scientists thought it was fake!

Platypus regularly hold their breath for two minutes to find food.

Platypus can hold their breath for about six minutes if hiding from a *predator*.

Platypus have no teeth! They have grinding pads made of the same material as horse hooves.

What do you call more than one platypus? Some call them platypus, platypi, or platypuses.

When disturbed or handled, platypus make a low growling sound.

Platypus Words

Bill: A soft, leathery snout that has electro-receptors to pick up on the small electrical signals sent by animals when they move. p5

Biofluorescent: Reflects bright colors when exposed to ultraviolet light (light that we can't see that comes from the sun). p7

Burrow: A hole or tunnel dug by a small animal, to be its home. p9

Captivity: Living in the care of humans. p28

Carnivore: An animal that only eats other animals. p19

Electroreception: The ability to detect electric fields and currents. p16

Foraging: Searching for food. p18

Habitat: The natural home of an animal. p25

Incubate: Keeping eggs at the right temperature so they will hatch. p24

Mammal: A warm-blooded, vertebrate animal which produces milk to feed its young and usually has fur. (Warm-blooded: An animal that usually keeps its body temperature at the same rate, even if its surroundings are hotter or colder; Vertebrate: An animal that has a backbone). p2

Monotreme: An egg-laying mammal, including the platypus and the echidna. p2

Near-Threatened: May become in danger of extinction without protection efforts. p25

Nocturnal: An animal that is mostly asleep during the day and awake at night. p17

Predator: Animal that eats other animals. p13

Puggles: Baby platypus! p25

Venomous: An animal that can inject venom by biting or stinging. p22

Ornithorhynchus anatinus

Learn More

What is a Platypus? | *National Ocean Service*
oceanservice.noaa.gov/facts/platypus.html

Platypus | *Encyclopedia Britannica*
www.britannica.com/animal/platypus

Platypus | *Australian Museum*
australian.museum/learn/animals/mammals/platypus/

Platypus | *San Diego Zoo Wildlife Explorers*
sdzwildlifeexplorers.org/animals/platypus

Made in the USA
Monee, IL
19 May 2024